A BOOK OF UNCOMMON FAITH

A Book of Uncommon Faith

KENNETH G. PHIFER

COMPILED AND EDITED BY

DOROTHY J. MARCHAL

UPPER ROOM BOOKS
NASHVILLE

A Book of Uncommon Faith

Published by Upper Room Books in 1991.

Cover Illustration and Design: Harriette Bateman
Book Design: Harriette Bateman
First Printing: April 1991 (7)
Library of Congress Catalog Card Number: 90-71862
ISBN: 0-8358-0632-4

Printed in the United States of America

THIS VOLUME IS DEDICATED

TO THE MEMORY OF

KENNETH AND PENNEY PHIFER

A song from a Broadway show assures us that on clear days we can see forever. I have few clear days. Some days are so unclear that I cannot see at all. Prayer can be a clearing of my eyes, a way of taking a long view. So I will pray.

K.G.P.

CONTENTS

FOREWORD

KENNETH PHIFER arrived in New Orleans in August 1965
to assume the senior pastorate of the St. Charles Avenue
Presbyterian Church. Shortly after his arrival the city was
devastated by Hurricane Betsy, and within the same month
Dr. Phifer suffered a heart attack. The city and Dr. Phifer
recovered, but both events foreshadowed a career in New
Orleans that included other shattering blows: an almost-fatal
car accident involving his younger son, his wife's struggle
against cancer and her subsequent invalidism, and his defeat
in a campaign to become the honorary chief executive of his
denomination. Such personal crises, along with the concerns
and responsibilities of his work, seemed only to strengthen
his faith. Although the years in New Orleans had their difficulties, Dr. and Mrs. Phifer enjoyed a rich and full ministry in
the Crescent City.

As his secretary for the eighteen years of his residence in
New Orleans, I had the privilege and good fortune to help him
in church matters and in manuscript preparation. At the time
of his death on November 1, 1985, the manuscript for *A Book
of Uncommon Faith* was partially complete. In this book of
prayers, as was true in *A Book of Uncommon Prayer,* I have
changed the prayers from their original prose form into free
verse. I have also revised and enlarged upon passages from his
introduction to his first book of prayers in order to shape the
book in a manner that I believe Dr. Phifer would approve.

The prayers that follow, although originally used in public

worship services, are personal meditations, as were the prayers in *A Book of Uncommon Prayer*. They are the thoughts of an extremely private person who could nonetheless express his innermost feelings for universal appeal. The prayers deal with anguish, despair, and heartache as well as with happiness, hope, and the beauty of all human experiences. They demonstrate Dr. Phifer's ability to savor and share the various times when he prayed.

I would like to express my appreciation to Dr. Phifer's family for its approval of and cooperation in the preparation of this manuscript. I would also commend my dear friend, the late Anna McPheeters, for her assistance and support. Her diligence and competence were exceeded only by her concern that this manuscript be published. My appreciation is also extended to Linda Hobson for her expertise in editing and evaluating the manuscript, especially for her suggestion regarding the cyclical form of the book. Faith goes in cycles, and the pattern in this book is learning, trying, failing, beginning again, then going out to act on God's will.

DOROTHY J. MARCHAL

INTRODUCTION

Running from God's the longest race of all.
—THEODORE ROETHKE

YEARS AGO I read a newspaper account of a man wanted for murder in a midwestern state who walked into a police station to give himself up. When asked why he surrendered, he answered with a shrug, "You can't run forever." Yet we keep on running, most of us. That is our way of life in America in this last part of the twentieth century. You are a runner if you are an average American. I am a runner. I realized it recently. Perhaps, in part because I am getting older, I see that I cannot run forever. Yet, paradoxically, changes in my personal life during the past few years have accelerated the pace at which I have run.

It all began to come together when my wife and I took a brief vacation, a scant two weeks, only forty miles from New Orleans on the Bogue Falaya River in southern Louisiana at a house borrowed from some friends. I am an habitual early riser, and each morning I found myself wandering down the slope to the bank of the river to sit on a hammock and watch the mists dissolve. For the first time in years, I felt no compulsion to turn on either radio or television to catch the news. For the first time in years (except on those frustrating mornings when the paper boy was late or did not show), I had no newspaper until I went to town to buy one. And for the first time in years, I was not driven to use those early hours to read something. I did not start the day running. I eased into it, taking one step at a time. I was in no hurry even to say a morning prayer.

Usually I am at my office by 8:15, and after I have had a few minutes of quiet at my desk, the day begins. The office staff arrives at 8:30. The telephone rings. There is a sound of bustle in the hall as the children gather for day school. Even in a church, we are all off and running. But not so on the banks of the Bogue Falaya. It is not much of a river. As a pine-darkened, deep South waterway, it seldom even has a current. Most of the time it just lies there, placid and still. In the morning, mullet jump and the small catfish swim near the surface, but for the most part, the Bogue Falaya just lies there. When I sat by it, my mind and spirit tended to lie there too, placid and quiet. That is the way it was for me, morning after morning. I had quit running, and only when I stopped did I realize how close to exhaustion I was.

For some time I had recognized that the edge of my creativity was blunted. Sermons had become a chore. Administration was a burden. Pastoral work left me emotionally depleted. I had lost any sense of the smooth pace of the long-distance runner. Life was a series of desperate sprints followed by periods of catching my breath before the next burst of effort. One cannot run that way forever. One must hit one's stride and pace oneself. I was finding now that I even had to slow down to walk. Sometimes one has to find some Bogue Falaya of one's own and sit on the bank, letting its serenity and peace pervade the spirit. That is hardest of all. There is so little time!

After the first morning or two of random thought and unguided contemplation, I began to "free associate" with some word of scripture or verse that came to mind. One day I found myself just asking God to help me with my confusion and depression. All day long that prayer kept coming back to me. When I began to grow anxious, I told myself that that was natural and I prayed again. When I fretted over some uncertainty or problem I knew I had to face when I got back to work, I realized my emotional and mental exhaustion.

Another morning some lines of poetry, packed away in my memory years ago, surfaced:

> God, when you thought of a pine tree,
> How did you think of a star?
> How did you think of clear brown pools
> Where flocks of shadows are?
>
> . . . .
>
> God, when you thought of a pine tree,
> How did you think of a star?

And as I looked up at the pine trees on the banks of the Bogue Falaya and at the river where the mullet jumped, I knew that was a pretty good question. How did God think of all these things? Because of that question, my head was on a little straighter all day long.

One morning as I sat in my hammock by the river, the first verse of Psalm 121 came to mind: "I lift up my eyes to the hills. From whence does my help come?" I tried to put the figure of speech into its Palestinian setting. A shepherd watches his flock. A lion appears. The shepherd is alone until he looks toward the hills where his friends appear, coming to help him drive the lion away. What created that figure of speech in which the delivering God appears outlined against the skyline, rushing to the aid of the people? Then I realized it did not matter what inspired so graphic a metaphor. God does come at a rush, appearing on the skyline when we lift our eyes. There are times in life down in some lonesome valley when we have had it, and we look up and out and beyond ourselves and something, someone, seems to be rushing down the slope toward us.

I lift up my eyes to the hills. From whence does my help come? All this means is that I am not on my own, no matter the circumstances. There is a dimension to life that is beyond me, that sometimes unexpectedly swoops down to my rescue. Or, perhaps, I do not need rescuing. Perhaps I just need some expanding. I am spending too much time at an old dried-up waterhole. This lifting up of the eyes and looking out can come at any time, anywhere. But for it to do so, it needs the discipline of some time, some place. I am convinced anew of the importance of a deliberate withdrawal into a quiet place for at least a brief, intense period. Howard Thurman has a phrase for it. He calls it "a centering moment." He means a focusing time, a zeroing in, a pivoting instant.

Very important to such a centering moment is the readiness to begin where we are. Most of us feel the need to develop a prayerful mood. Yet there is another side to the matter. Elijah spoke to his God out of a blue funk one day, sitting under a broom tree and asking that he might die, telling the Lord bluntly: "It is enough; now, O Lord, take away my life; for I am no better than my fathers" (1 Kings 19:4). Jeremiah went at God, hammer and tongs, accusingly:

> I sat alone, because thy hand was upon me,
>   for thou hadst filled me with indignation.
> Why is my pain unceasing,
>   my wound incurable,
>   refusing to be healed?
> Wilt thou be to me like a deceitful brook,
>   like waters that fail?
>   Jeremiah 15:17-18

Yet somehow prayer which begins this honestly leaves us very close to God when we have finished. Job's querulous, complaining impatience brought him to the place where he could say: "I had heard of thee by the hearing of the ear, / but now my eye sees thee" (Job 42:5). Meanwhile his friends, who had shushed his bitter defiance, faded into the colorless background of their unimaginative orthodoxy.

The truest mark of prayer is the depth of feeling that generates it. That feeling may be anger or hurt, doubt or despair, exuberance or gratitude. It is said that one day on a journey of mercy Saint Teresa of Avila stood mired in mud. She cried out to God: "If this is the way you treat your friends, no wonder you don't have many."

Prayer is very personal, but it is interpersonal, too, and always involves others. It comes at times unbidden. It can be a place of ordering, a place where everything is brought together in the presence of God, who helps sort it all out. Prayer is a look within and a look without. It is the matching of an inner need with an outward-reaching hope.

Sometimes prayer is quietness and peace. Sometimes it is a loud crying out and a clamorous calling as though God did not know that we are here. Sometimes it is in the company of others in a service of worship—a common prayer. Sometimes it is in the privacy of our homes.

Trust in God is central to our faith. What do we mean by a word such as *faith?* Do we not mean, in part at least, prayer?

Prayer is not just words. It is the shape of a moment in which we acknowledge God, who is more than the moment. Our words are an effort to give content to the moment. We often pray for things we should work for, and we work for things we should pray for. Sorting out the differences is not easy.

Prayer is a way of paying attention, of centering the self again, of putting things in place. There are all kinds of prayers—routine, spontaneous, formal, sudden, ceremonial. God hears them all.

K. G. P.

Learning to Pray

I GIVE THANKS FOR PRAYER

At times we pray because we must.
At times we pray because we feel we ought.
At times we pray because it is time.
So now I pray.

Eternal God, I give you thanks
   for the privilege of prayer,
   for the times I pray because I must,
Because I am lonely and fear-filled,
   at the end of my tether,
   battered and broken.
I pray at such hours,
   only half believing in my prayers.
And yet, I have known an insurgent strength
   and reassurance that came anyhow.
I have prayed out of duty,
   routinely and uninspiredly.
Yet I have been surprised by joy
   in my routine repetitions,
And I have known that they turned out for good.
I have prayed by the clock,
And even then some sudden realization has come
   that you are near.
Time has been suspended,
And I have felt eternity pressing in upon me.

I give thanks for the privilege of prayer.
I become careless about it,
    indifferent to it,
    uncertain how to pray;
And yet, I would not give it up,
    for I know prayer is at the heart of faith.

And so I pray this day for myself,
    with my secret frets and fears,
    my carefully concealed feelings,
    and my strongly repressed emotions.
I pray for renewed faith and hope,
    so that my daily life may sparkle
    more than it ordinarily does.
I pray that I may be someone
    for whom purpose and direction are realities.
I pray for ever-deepening relationships
    with those I love,
And ever-broadening relationships that will include
    those whom I might love if I knew them.

I thank you, O God,
    that I can pray.
Let me never feel that prayer is a last resort.
How marvelous it is as a first resort!
And so let me go about my days
    with prayer still upon my heart,
That I may live prayerfully,
    spontaneously,
And gladly in Christ, my Lord.   *Amen.*

WE NEED TO LEARN ACCEPTANCE

O Lord God,
You have made us for communion with one another
   and with you.
You intended us to break the silence with words
   and to bridge the gaps between us with language.
You taught us the uses of speech
   so that we can set our heartbreaks
     to the music of poetry
   and frame our hatred in curses.
We can say "I love you" to another human being,
And drive away a brother by saying "I hate you."
We are not always conscious of our own power,
For we use words so constantly—
   sometimes to build up,
   sometimes to break down,
   sometimes to hide behind.
Now we are trying to pray to you,
   Creator of the Universe,
Not knowing what words to use.

How are we to pray about our anxieties and fears?
Do we say, "Take them away, O Lord,
   and make us brave and confident"?
Are we willing to let them go,
   to launch them in trust?
How are we to pray about our hostilities?
Do we say, "Make me loving and kind"?

Do we want to be loving and kind
  when it may mean abandoning
  our posture of injured righteousness?
How are we to pray for our brothers and sisters?
Do we dare pray what we feel?

What are we to do about so many areas of life?
Do we just go on using the proper words, like
  "Forgive us our sins
  as we forgive those who sin against us"?
If words are real and not just a formula,
We are in trouble.
For it is not just the people in other countries,
  with whom we cannot agree,
  that we do not want to forgive;
It is the upsetting people around us,
  even a member of the family or a neighbor.

Lord, we had best refrain from speaking.
For we still have a lot of uncertainty.
But, O Lord,
Please do not forgive us
  only to the extent we can forgive others.
Teach us not just what to say
  but how to live.
In Jesus Christ our Lord.   *Amen.*

A MORNING PRAYER

O Lord, in the morning thou dost hear my voice.

Good morning.

But is it a good morning?
I had a restless night,
   and I have a day before me that I dread.
I did not rest well,
   and I don't eagerly anticipate the hours ahead.
Sometimes I fear the coming hours,
   sometimes I face them with calm serenity;
Sometimes I fall in between.
But wherever I fall,
I think about where a long-ago psalmist found himself:
"O Lord, in the morning thou dost hear my voice;
   in the morning I . . . watch."

Whether I feel anxious or eager,
   expecting nothing or ready for anything,
This is a good time to say something of my own to God.
It may be very simple and direct, that word.
It need not be profound but natural,
   not complex but easy.
It may be a shoulder-squaring word, like
   "This day I go forth in the strength of the Lord."
That can be a tone-setting sentence
   if I really let myself feel that I do go forth
     in the strength of the Lord.
I will say it now and remind myself throughout the day
     that I said it and meant it.
And watch!

I will look about me at the beginning of the day,
Stop long enough to get my head on straight,
   to take in some sense of the Presence of God.
A song declares that "On a clear day you can see forever."
I have seldom had that experience,
But I have often found that on any kind of a day,
   clear or murky,
   sunshine or rainy,
I can see a step or two ahead
   if I stop and draw a breath or two
   and wait a moment or two,
And ask God to point me in the right direction.

So, good morning.
It can be a good morning
   because each morning is a new beginning,
   each day a fresh start.
I will go with God.   *Amen.*

I NEED PERSPECTIVE IN MY PRAYERS

When you cannot pray as you should,
pray as you can.
                        —A WISE SAYING

Eternal God,
How should I pray?
I do not really know.
My prayers are so fashioned by my desires
    and so entangled with my needs and hopes and fears
I must confess,
I do not know how to pray.
Perhaps, O Lord, that is how I should pray—
    out of myself,
    my true self,
    my self of need and hope and fear,
    my deep-down self of confusion and complexity.
So I pray as I can.
I hold up those inner things
    that matter so much to me now.
You know what they are, for you know me.
I pray as I can.
Where there is a problem,
    give me perspective.
Where there is anxiety,
    relax my tension.
Where there is guilt,
    remind me that there is forgiveness.
Where there is resentment,
    keep me from the dark bitterness
    that makes all of life taste sour.
Love me into loving.

I know, too, that only through fear and insecurity
    do I avoid the confrontations of love.
I am uneasy in my intimacies,
    unsure in my casual relationships with others.
I fail to listen to their needs,
    so concerned am I with concealing my own.
My life reflects the world of men and women
    who war and wrangle and hate.
I ask peace for myself and for others.
I ask for true beginnings of reciprocal good will,
That in the give and take of discussion and debate
    may come new visions and new hope,
    the strengthening of the will to freedom,
    and mutual respect among all peoples.
For all these things,
    large and small,
I pray in Christ's name. *Amen.*

I HAVE BEEN TWO-FACED

Lord God,
I am back again in a posture of prayer
   with words of praise and supplication.
I often act as though you did not hear me
   the last time I prayed.
I say the same things over and over.
I repeat the same petitions.
Maybe I did not hear myself,
Simply said things by rote
   and had done with it.
I have asked for your Spirit in my heart
And then have gone forth to act and think and feel
   just as I was accustomed to doing,
With never a pause to wonder
   whether I was acting, thinking, and feeling
   in accord with the Spirit for which I prayed.
I have asked to be forgiven,
   affirming blandly my own readiness to forgive.
Then I have gone forth to speak my sour words at home
   and my angry words at work.

I have praised gentle Jesus
   and then have acted meanly.
I have exalted the heart of compassion and love
And then have let the curdled milk of my lovelessness
   spill over into the lives of others.
I have brought my own hurts to you
   and have vented my frustrations upon others.

I have prayed for all humankind
and then have expressed contempt for a neighbor.
I cannot in all honesty be very proud of myself.

But then, O Lord,
You do not ask that I come with pride,
in shining garments of my own righteousness.
You just ask that I come.
So I offer the same old prayers:
I want your Spirit in my life.
I want to be forgiven.
I look to Jesus
as the one who exemplifies love and life.
I want to be more loving,
more sensitive,
more aware of others.
I cannot make any promises,
But if you will touch me now with your finger,
and lay your healing, helpful hand upon me,
I will be grateful;
and out of my gratitude I will respond to life.
If you heal my hurts,
I can be more receptive to the hurts of others.
If you forgive me, I can forgive others.
If you love me, I can be more loving.
I may fail at times
and have to ask for renewal,
But I cannot be careless or callous or indifferent.

I am still and waiting.
For what, sometimes, I am not sure.
But I have prayed and soon I shall pray again—
   the same words,
   the same petitions,
   the same fears and doubts.
Thank you, O God, for the feeling of your nearness.
I may lose that feeling before this day is done,
   but draw me back again and again,
So that life may be increasingly permeated
   with the joy of your Presence.
Let each day beckon me to new experiences
And each day call me to new opportunities,
In Jesus Christ our Lord. *Amen.*

I NEED PRODDING

Because prayer is so many things, our Father,
I am in a quandary about how to begin.
Shall I say,
   "Holy, Holy, Holy!
   Lord God Almighty!
   Early in the morning
     our song shall rise to thee,"
And then wait,
   reveling in thanksgiving,
   rejoicing in praise?
Shall I cry,
   "O Lord, my needs are great,
   my strength small;
   do what seems best"?
Then shall I fall silent with the hope
   that some great manifestation
   of the power of the Spirit will seize me?

How shall I begin?
Shall I just declare,
   "Lord, I am grateful,
     but I know not how to say it.
   I am in need,
     but I know not how to ask for help.
   I am anxious to know the experience of prayer,
     but I do not know what
     the experience of prayer really means"?

I have never seen a blinding light,
    never beheld a vision,
    never heard an angel speak.
So I shall simply be quiet
    and let my thoughts go where they will.

I think of myself, quite naturally.
But is that wrong?
I have been told you are concerned for me,
    for my limited loves,
    my caged-up life.
I have my own problems and doubts.
I have secrets I prefer not to mention.
Do you know about them
    and what they mean to me?
Of course you do, O Lord,
    for you know my inmost heart.
Help me to understand myself.
I have places of which I am ashamed.
Do you know about them?
Even in phrasing the question,
    I realize how foolish it is.
Of course you do.
Does the fact that you know me at my best
        and at my worst,
    and still accept me,
    mean that I can accept myself?
Can I quit trying to hide,
    quit trying to fool myself and others?
Can I take off my mask?
Is that when prayer begins,
    when I unmask and say,

"Here I am, O Lord,
    please listen"?

Let the beginning not be the ending.
Keep me moving along in prayer.
Keep me from being afraid of life.
Keep me from being afraid of joy.
Keep me, too, from being afraid of sorrow.
Just keep me, Lord, through Jesus Christ.   *Amen.*

FOR AN AWARENESS OF THE SPIRIT

The wind blows where it wills, and you hear the
sound of it.

—JOHN 3:8

O God, Redeemer,
Unto you I lift my prayer,
From you I seek forgiveness,
And by you I would dedicate myself
   to better things and nobler living.
I thank you for all the ways you do come to me—
   in the large and the small things of life,
   in the joys and sorrows of daily experience.
I have not always heeded your coming.
I have not always been aware of you.
Let this morning prayer be a means
   of so clarifying my vision today
That I may at least glimpse you
   as you come to me tomorrow.

Perhaps you will come in a song,
Perhaps in a tear,
Perhaps in the hearty laughter that bubbles
   from the pure mind of a child.
Perhaps I shall know your coming
   by an opportunity to be kind.
The important thing, O Lord,
   is that your Spirit enter my heart
      to make me know you are always near,
      very near.

Teach me to live with the awareness
That enables me to present unto you each hour of my life,
    polished by gracious living.
Let me hold my head high in the face of woe and loss.
Let me declare unceasing war upon temptation and evil.
Let me bear banners of songs against discouragement and
    despair.
Let me keep an open mind,
    a sense of humor,
    a reverent spirit,
And let me always be a little kinder than necessary.

These, above all else, are the gifts I would ask.
For if my spirit is serene,
    my body will be healthier.
If my mind is composed,
    my task will be more efficiently accomplished.
If my heart is sure,
    my hand will be steadier.
So make me clean and pure within.
Re-create me in the very center of my being.

As I am re-created,
May I help re-create a little of the world around me.
The outer world reflects the inner turmoil of others.
There is no peace in the world
    because there is so little peace within me.
I struggle and strain,
I puff and pull,
I pant and then collapse, breathless, before my problem.
Because I have not allowed myself
    to see the answers to my difficulties,
I believe there are no answers.

Ah, forgive me for such a faulty assumption.
Let me be humble enough to see
   that while there is no answer in me,
There is the great answer in Christ.   *Amen.*

I AM AWKWARD AT PRAYER

The spirit is hesitant,
And the words come haltingly
   when I come to the time of prayer,
For I do not know how to pray.
Let me try.
Let me pray.

O Lord, my God,
My glibness deserts me,
My facility of expression flees.
I am uncertain, timid, even afraid.
I am perplexed as to what is expected of me.
How should I pray,
   and what should I say?
I am fearful at the thought of launching out in faith
   with the expectation I shall really be heard.
I am afraid to be myself.
I bring myself to prayer all stiff and starched,
My will pressed and my intentions freshly ironed;
So stiff with piety and so starched with high purpose
   that I am not entirely comfortable.
I speak a language I do not ordinarily use,
   and I carefully launder my feelings.
Lord, why do I pose and posture?
You must see through me.
You must know me as I am.

I know that the whole glad message of the gospel
Lies in the news that you have come in Jesus Christ
       our Lord.

You have shown your love for me
  in that while I was yet a sinner,
Christ died for me.
I have heard that word proclaimed again and again.
Give me the openness to receive it
  and the grace to live it.
Give me the freedom to celebrate it
  and the confidence to come to you
In the assurance that your mercy is great enough
  to encompass all my needs.

My needs, I know,
  reflect the needs of everyone.
My anger is the anger
  that divides people from one another.
My resentment is the kind
  that causes us to destroy our neighbors.
I am not as different as I like to pretend I am.
So when I ask for your forgiveness,
  I must forgive.
When I demand mercy,
  I must show mercy.
When I affirm faith in your grace,
  I must live graciously.
You know, O Lord God,
  this is not always easy for me to do.
Will you help me speak words that need to be spoken
  and do things that need to be done?

Let me face the days that are ahead
  with courage and confidence in the future,
  with thankfulness for all the good things
    I have known and experienced,
  with joy even amid tears.
That, where I am and as I am,
  I live in your keeping.
I give myself into that keeping
  through Jesus Christ my Lord.   *Amen.*

Times of Seeking

UNFAITH BUILDS NO CATHEDRALS

O God of all,
I am grateful for the assurance
    that I call faith.
For I realize that it is by my faith
    that life is expanded and widened.
When I sink into unfaith,
    I am crabby and cranky and depressed.
Unfaith builds no cathedrals,
    sings no songs.
Unfaith never reaches,
    never hopes,
        never dares.
Unfaith walks alone,
    weeps alone.
Unfaith is dark,
Faith is bright.

Faith stares into the shadows
    and sees the form and shape of hope.
It peers into the unknown
    and sees the promise of meaning.
It liberates and frees me,
And that is what I want, O Lord.
I want life that is abundant
    and peace that passes understanding
        in the midst of this tossing, tumultuous world.
Give me faith, I pray,
    the kind of faith our Lord Jesus exemplifies.

I am small when I stand alongside him—
  that I readily admit.
But I grow taller as I walk with him—
  that feeling I earnestly desire.
Give me some measure of his confidence and courage,
  his joy and his gladness.
Give me hands like his with which to touch other lives—
  healing hands, strong hands.
Give me words like his to speak—
  words weighted with your love
    and the power of faith.
Give me eyes like his to see beauty amid ugliness,
  dignity amid despair.
Give me the staying power he showed
  in situations of stress,
And the flexibility he manifested
  in the midst of flux and change.
Give me a vision like his so that I can see
  beyond the moment to eternity,
So that I may look through time
  to those realities that endure.
Go with me, I pray,
As I go with Jesus along the crowded ways of life.   *Amen.*

I BRING MYSELF TO YOU

It's all I have to bring today,
This, and my heart beside.
—EMILY DICKINSON

Eternal God,
In you I live and move and have my being.
So often, I confess, I forget that elemental fact
    about you and about myself.
I feel lost, estranged,
    as though I live here on earth,
While you dwell in some far-off heaven,
    looking down upon me, your child, at play.
Life becomes unreal to me,
    and I plod along joylessly and doggedly.
Yet deep inside me, I know
    that in you I live and move and have my being.

That is the reason I am here today.
I want to get back in touch,
    for I have known that lost feeling in recent days.
I want a renewed sense of belonging.
I want to keep in touch,
    and this act of worship is important to me.
I have felt the Presence.
I have felt a sustaining power when I needed it.
I have felt that I was supported
    when my own will sagged
    and my spirit went limp.

I have been propped up on my leaning side
   when temptation came.
I need to keep in touch with you, O Lord.

Pressures of all kinds threaten me.
It is so easy for me to give in to secondhand living,
   to secondhand values,
   second-rate pleasures,
   and shopworn indulgences.
So I bring all that I have today—
   my hopes and fears,
   my joys and sorrows,
   my faith and doubts.
I bring them and my heart beside,
   for receiving and refreshing
   and reviving in worship and in prayer.
In Jesus' name, I pray. *Amen.*

FOR A TIME OF LONELINESS

Better is a neighbor who is near
than a brother who is far away.
—PROVERBS 27:10

O Lord, I so often walk empty streets.
There are no greetings from the dark,
   no lazy sounds of murmured conversations
    among people whose faces I cannot see
   but whose voices, when raised in laughter, I know.
I am grateful for the cool comfort of my home
   against the steamy, strength-sapping,
    Southern summer nights.
I would not give it up,
   fling wide my doors and windows.
But I am wistful at times for voices out of the dark,
   for murmured conversations and easy laughter in the
    distance.
I enter the cool,
   shut out the night,
   lock my doors against the menace
    of intruders from the dark,
And sit, pensive, in my comfort.

Help me to find ways to hear others
   over the hum of air conditioners,
   above the flow of traffic.
Alert my senses to the smell of jasmine blossoms
    on the night breeze,
   lest I forget they are there

And sniff only the sterile, empty scent
 of my cut-flower arrangements,
 here today and gone tomorrow.
I remember Jesus and his field lilies and his friends.

I am lonely.
I think I shall walk the street again,
 look at the empty porches in the night
 and listen.
Someone may greet me and ask me to sit awhile.
If they do, I shall go with a prayer of gratitude.   *Amen.*

I SEEK MEANING IN LIFE

I come unto you, O God, with my morning prayers
Because you called me and I heard your call.
I heard even when
   I did not know it was your voice.
I have been moved by the promptings of habit,
   by the pressure of a sense of duty,
   by the fact that someone said,
"Let's go to church today."
These are but surface things, I know,
   and my response may have been shallow.
But beneath habit, duty, idle curiosity,
I know that in us all
   there is the quest for life and meaning.
I cannot always isolate the quest or name it,
And perhaps at times I do not recognize it.
But I want life to mean something
   and that involves you finally.
I want a sense of direction
   and that involves you finally.
I want some steadiness in my confusion,
   some guidance in my perplexity,
      and that involves you finally.

Sometimes I may find it hard
   to give in to my need for you.
I fight myself.
I am angry with you
   because I am angry with myself.

I am uncertain of you
    because I am uncertain of myself.
I have broken relationships with others,
    and that makes me feel the whole world is broken.
Mend me, O God,
    for you are the great healer.
Unite me with others, O Redeemer,
    for you are the great reconciler.
I ask not to be lulled or soothed
I ask but to be made whole.

Thank you for your refusal to leave me alone
    and for the ways in which I find myself
        unable to escape you finally.
Thank you for the promptings of habit and duty
    and for the disciplines of life that teach me,
    at last, that I cannot stand alone,
And that I do not need to stand alone.
There is the Lord Jesus Christ
    in whose name I pray.   *Amen.*

THE EVIDENCES OF YOUR LOVE

I am surrounded, O God,
   with so many evidences of your love
   and of the love of other human beings,
And I am grateful.
Help me in my sharing,
Help me in my living,
Help me in my hope,
Help me in my faith,
   that I may grow to a deeper understanding
     of the glory
Which is revealed through Jesus Christ our Lord. *Amen.*

THE MYSTERY AND THE GLORY

O God,
The mystery and the glory are the very essence of life.
I am not always aware of that.
Sometimes I am awed by the mystery,
  overwhelmed by it.
Sometimes I am uplifted on wings of glory.
Sometimes I just plod along,
  asking what it all means,
Sometimes it is only as I look back
  that I see meaning,
And I am grateful for it.
Sometimes out of the corners of my eyes,
I catch a glimpse of something so splendid
  that I am moved to inner tears.
Sometimes I know that the minor blessings
  that I so take for granted
    are really major miracles.
Sometimes I fumble in the dark
  for a God who seems to hide.
Sometimes I am sure,
  quite sure,
That the whole world is alive with signs of God's Presence.
I know then that I belong,
That I am held
  when I have no strength to hold myself,
That I am guided
  when I feel that I am lost.
The mystery and the glory are the very essence of life.
Thank you, O Lord, for that.   *Amen.*

O GOD, WHO NEVER SLEEPS

O Lord,
You are the one who never sleeps,
For whom the long watches of the night are as day
    and the darkness is as light.
Was it not said that your eye is on the sparrow
    and none falls to the ground without your notice?
Give me quiet confidence in my wakefulness
    and, in your care, watch over me now.
Some of us must not sleep
    for we are responsible for some part of the city's life.
Some of us cannot sleep
    for we are restless and anxious,
        our minds racing,
        our thoughts circling,
        our bodies rigid.

Be present with those of us who must not sleep,
    guarding us and guiding us in your wakefulness.
If we have tasks to do,
    give us alertness and diligence.
Keep us in your keeping until the morning light.
Be present with those of us who cannot sleep.
Still our racing minds and relax our tumbling spirits.
Soothe our troubled hearts and quiet our restless tossing.
For was it not also said of you,
        "God gives his beloved sleep"?
You are our strength in conquering the dark,
    the dark about us and the dark within.

Let the darkness about us be a kind darkness,
   which comes from you
      to shut out the turmoil and the toil of the day.
Let the darkness within us
   give way to the light of your Presence
   and the sun of your salvation,
Until all the night is bright with the joy of your nearness
   and our restless hearts give thanks.
You are our hope of victory until the morning comes
   and the shadows fall away.
Encircle us now with a sense
   of the friendliness of the night,
Like a soft, dark cape with the beauty of stillness and
      calm.

O God, who never sleeps,.
Be with us now
   and in the hours that lie ahead.   *Amen.*

FOR A TIME OF SEEKING

Who has known the mind of the Lord,
or who has been his counselor?
—ROMANS 11:34

Who are you, O Lord?
God Almighty,
Creator of Heaven and Earth,
Lord and Giver of Life,
Ancient of Days,
Lord Sabaoth your name.
Like others, I use such forms of address,
But I am not sure that they mean very much
    in the deep places of my experience.
They are handles
    whereby we humans grasp at your mystery
        and your meaning.
But when dark hours come,
    when pain takes over,
    when despair threatens to overwhelm,
None of us is sure that your titles mean very much.
When life sings,
    when the senses are alive and vibrant,
    when we feel the thrill of being,
We cannot capture the mystery in words
    or exhaust the meaning
By defining you in abstract terms.

Who are you, O Lord?
None of us really knows.
We know only that at times
    a sound,
    a silence,
    a song,
    a splendor,
    a sob,
    a star
May intrude upon our routine.
And we are aware,
        suddenly aware,
That you are.

How do we name you?
Can we know you?
Can we claim you?
Can I?
My imagination falters.

And then I turn back to a word spoken long ago in Galilee,
    to a man who was both mystery and meaning,
    to a life that was lived,
    to a death that was suffered,
    to a resurrection that was accomplished.
And I know that in him is an answer
    and a whole series of new questions.
The answer lies in his grasp of life,
    his grace,
    his love,
    his concern,
    his indomitable faith.
The questions come as I wonder about myself.

Can I be at all like him?
Is he too much for any of us?
Are his dreams too big
   and his love too great for us?
Then I remember how he said,
   "Whosoever will, let him come."
And I dare to set my feet on the pathway to hope.
Am I like him?
Am I right to think of the light of the knowledge of your
            glory
   as revealed in his face?
Can I cast aside my fears and my self-depreciation enough
   to believe you care for all of us as we are?
I believe I can by your grace,
Through Jesus Christ our Lord.   *Amen.*

I SEEK MERCY

Eternal Father,
You have made us for yourself,
And apart from you we are never truly satisfied.
In you alone is fullness of joy and peace forevermore.
Hear me as I pray.

Be my vision
    that I may see what is truly good in life.
Be my courage
    that I may faithfully pursue it.
Be my fortress
    in the hour of temptation,
    a house of defense to save me from myself.
Be my light
    when the day is dark
    and I know not which way to turn.
Be my strength
    when I am weak
    and my spirit is troubled and distressed.
Be my assurance
    when those I love are taken from my sight
    and you alone can uphold and comfort me.
Be my hope
    when my own hopes fail
    and, but for you, I should give way to despair.
Be at all times my help and my salvation.
Until at length by your great mercy,
I win the victory over sin and death
    and come to everlasting life
        through Jesus Christ our Lord. *Amen.*

I SEEK YOUR HELP

Out of the disconnected events of everyday experience,
  O God,
Help me to form a pattern of understanding.
Help me to seek a direction.
Help me to commit myself to purpose and meaning.
I know that these are the most significant things for me.
Help me to know that I must hold fast
  to what I understand is good.
Help me to know
    that I cannot vacillate,
    trying to serve two masters.
Help me to know, finally,
    that in the glory that comes to me
        through Jesus Christ,
There is meaning for life—
    direction,
    purpose,
    strength. *Amen.*

I ASK FOR SO MUCH

Almighty God,
I come to you in prayer with confidence
   because you have bid me come
And because, in my seeking and searching,
   you always meet me more than halfway.
I come with timidity
   because, I have heard,
You meet those who quest along the way.
I come with gladness
   because life has been sweet and rich.
I come, sometimes with a dour countenance,
   because life has been a nagging headache
      and daily existence has gone sour.
I come with all kinds of moods
   and with all sorts of problems.
When I am bold and confident,
   renew my faith in life;
But keep me cautiously skeptical about myself.
When I am timid,
   create respect in me for myself.
Give me a trust in life
   and a sense of worth to you.
Erase from my spirit those dark splotches of despair
   and from my heart those black streaks of rejection.
Give me the courage to accept your love,
For, I confess,
It does take more courage than I sometimes possess.
I look upon life and am appalled.
I see so many evidences of wrong.

I look upon love and am afraid.
To give love makes me vulnerable to hurt
    and to accept love lays demands upon me.
Yet, for all my fears and doubts,
I keep returning to this place of worship.
I know that whatever answers there are
    to life's problems and perplexities
    must come from beyond me.

So give me faith in the presence of my difficulties
    and renewed joy amid my uncertainties.
Give me good will toward others,
And take from me the predilection
    to quick judgment and easy labeling,
Whereby I dismiss my brothers and sisters.
Deliver me from isolation
    in a world hungry for communion and fellowship.
Deliver me from starched self-righteousness
    in a world limp from a lack of compassion and mercy.
Deliver me from smug assurance of my own rectitude
    in a world so desperately in need of reconciliation.

I pray for all who minister in your name.
And for myself I pray
    that I may become a minister of hope
        and a herald of reconciliation.
Hear my prayer and grant me peace,
Through Jesus Christ. *Amen.*

I SEEK PEACE

Come to me, all who labor and are heavy laden,
and I will give you rest.

—MATTHEW 11:28

The labor of another week is gone, O Lord.
Its weariness is behind me.
Its failures are done
   and its successes accomplished.
I come to you now in prayer.
I lift my heart to you.
I beseech your blessing.
Be very near to me.
Be close to my heart.

I come, O God, with my varying needs
   and different attitudes.
Sometimes I come joyously
   because life is good—
   my cup is full
     and my rejoicing runneth over.
Sometimes I come in despair
   because now it seems to my eyes
   life is not good,
   hope is but a forlorn dream,
     and faith is a mockery.
Sometimes I come in sorrow—
   some expectation has proven vain,
   some hope has been defeated and overthrown,
   some loved one has hurt my heart
     or I have hurt theirs.

Sometimes I come indifferently—
    I have not expected much
        and have not been disappointed.
Sometimes I come with the harsh memory
        of a recently committed sin
        thrusting itself into my mind.
I am thankful that you welcome me
        however I come—
    with dust-stained soul,
    with careless heart,
    even with flippant thoughts.
You have a word to speak to my heart
If I but listen,
If I but believe.

O Ever Blessed God,
    you hear my prayers.
You know my needs.
You are gracious to forgive
    and have plenteous mercy.
You bless me even when I know it not.
For I am your perplexed and bewildered child, O God,
    uncertain of myself
    and all too often secretly uncertain of you.
But you are sure,
And you take the intent for the deed,
    the aspiration for the accomplishment.
Draw me now unto you.

Help my feet to gain the certain way.
When I falter,
    renew my strength.
When I am fearful,
    inspirit me.
When I am weak,
    restore me.
For you alone are the eternal goodness
    in whom I can trust.
So unto you I commit myself,
    through Jesus Christ our Lord.   *Amen.*

I SEEK TO SERVE

Eternal God,
How far beyond me you are, it seems,
   as I name you and pray to you.
To say "God" opens boundless vistas
   of power and grandeur.
It conjures up visions
   of that which is limitless and inscrutable,
   of mystery beyond inference,
   of wisdom beyond comprehension.
Yet even as I acknowledge you with awe
   and confess my finiteness with humility,
I hear the Lord Jesus saying "Father,"
And suddenly I know that you are close to me,
   that you compress infinity into recognizable boundaries,
   and incomprehensibility into terms I can grasp.
For Jesus I am grateful,
   for his walking among us,
   for his long-ago life in Galilee,
   for his present spirit in my heart and life.
As I look back to him,
Let me look around also
So that he comes alive
   to dwell among us as the Word made flesh.

May he come alive as Savior and Redeemer,
As the one who touches life where I am sore,
Renews life where I am jaded and frustrated
   and heals broken places.

May he come alive as Lord,
As the one whose claim upon me
   gives courage for times of strain,
   faith for the carrying forward of responsibilities,
   love for providing dimension and depth to experience.
I confess I use his name carelessly,
   fling it about lightly.
I do not always take him as seriously as I pretend.
I excuse myself by saying that I am only human.
Then I realize what he made of humanness,
How he made life glow,
   love shine,
   hope gleam,
And I am ashamed very often of doing so little
   with the life given me.

So I pray, O God, for the kind of glad engagement
   with others and with you
That removes the shoddiness and the shabbiness
   with which I sometimes rest content.
Lift me into service of the sort that reflects the love of
         Christ.
Draw me to the faith that shows the commitment of Christ.
Lead me by the hope that shines in the dark
   as his hope shone.   *Amen.*

FOR A TIME OF RESTLESSNESS

Rejoice always, pray constantly, give thanks in all circumstances; for this is the will of God in Christ Jesus for you.

— 1 THESSALONIANS 5:16-18

O God, who never sleeps,
For whom the watches of the night are as day
  and for whom the midnight is as noon,
Be with this sleepless one now.
Let me feel that you are near.
Sometimes I am wakeful by choice;
At other times I cannot find the blessings of sleep and rest.
There have been times when I have known
  the pain of bodily affliction
  or the ache of emotional unease.
I think back to the yesterday that is gone,
  with its good times
  and its not-so-good times.
I might have made it better
  if I had been more sensitive,
    more alert,
    more perceptive,
    more kind.
I would do some things over if I had the chance.
Yet I do have the chance to do some things over.
There is tomorrow yet to come.
There are relationships I can repair
  with a word of affection.

There are circumstances I can alter
   and situations I can transform.
Each day is a morning of creation.
Each morning I begin anew
   to put myself and my life together again.
Now, O Lord, as I wait,
   as I rest and relax before the morning comes,
Still me and quiet me
   with the unlimited resources of your care for me.

I know, too,
   there are some things I cannot do over.
Yesterday is gone.
And for those parts of yesterday's happenings
   that are irreparable or final,
Give me the willingness to accept what is over.
For errors or sin on my part,
   I am sorry,
But keep me from rejecting your forgiveness.
You have said
   whoever will, let that one come,
And here I am asking to be let in
   where the light of your love shines
   and the splendor of your mercy surrounds me,
      renews me,
      and gives me peace.
As the new morning dawns,
   clothe me in the armor of your light,
And go with me into the day
   that I may walk with confidence in love.   *Amen.*

I SEEK INSIGHT

I ask, O Lord, for eyes
   to recognize the contemporary meaning
     of the risen Christ.
I cannot see him with my eyes
   or touch him with my hands
   or hold him in my tight, hot, little fists.
But I can know the celebration of living,
   the feeling of new love,
   the meaning of deeper understanding.
I can know the power of the Spirit.
I can.
Help me, O Lord, through Jesus Christ our Lord. *Amen.*

I NEED UPLIFTING

My God and my Father,
Keep me from being afraid of my feelings.
Keep me from looking with suspicion
    upon the joyous, exuberant moments that
        sometimes come.
Keep me from being afraid to be happy.
Keep me from a dour doubting
    of the splendor of forgiveness.
Keep me from giving in to cynicism about our world
    and from yielding to hopelessness about the future.
Keep me from being so unrealistic
    that I refuse to admit evil,
        either in myself or in others.
And, at the same time,
Keep me from being so indifferent
    as to deny your redemptive grace,
        either in myself or in others.
Keep me from forgetting that this is your world,
And that I am your child.

I recognize, O Lord, that I face hours of special need
    when I cannot keep balance.
I am tipped over into despair
    because of the death of someone I love.
I wobble anxiously along
    through a period of tension and uncertainty.
I feel rejection by someone who matters to me.
You understand my special problems,

And I believe you do not demand more of me than I can
  give.
I am grateful that when I am unfaithful,
  you are loyal.
When I am unloving,
  you are compassionate.
When I stumble,
  you are merciful.
Of whom shall I be afraid?
Not of you, O God,
  not of you.
Awed, silenced, reverent,
  stilled by the magnificence of your love
  as manifested in Jesus Christ our Lord,
But not afraid!

So boldly I come, saying,
"O God, Rock and Salvation,
Hear me as I pray." *Amen.*

I NEED COURAGE

O Lord, you keep coming back to me,
   offering me freedom—
     freedom to live,
     freedom to be—
And I keep being frightened by your coming.
I ask that I may have enough courage,
   enough faith,
   enough trust in life,
To respond to the meaning of the Lord Jesus
     Christ. *Amen.*

Times of Weakening

I TURN TO YOU

O Lord God,
   unto whom I turn now in prayer and praise,
I want to be a stronger person.
I seek powers equal to my tasks.
I pray to come confidently into your Presence,
   holding up my life for your approval.
I want to bring you my proud accomplishments,
   show you my morning face and my eager heart,
And go forth pleased and satisfied.

But somehow, O Creator,
   it is not usually that way.
I have sought an easy life,
   and I have matched my tasks to my powers.
I must confess that I have preferred
   not to strain the muscles of my spirit
   nor to stretch the sinews of my heart.
I have avoided speaking out for that which is right and just
   because I did not want to be involved in controversy.
I have walked carefully down the middle of the road,
   lest I find some broken human being along the way.
I even have gone to church to give thanks
   that I am not like others—
      lazy, shiftless, improvident, and immoral—
And then I have gone home feeling justified.

I have asked you to use me in your service—
    within limits;
To take my silver and gold—
    sparingly;
To warm my heart and steel my will—
    carefully and with moderation.
You know me, Lord,
    far better than I know myself.
You know I do not want to be unloving,
    but I am afraid to be loving;
I may be hurt or betrayed.

I do not want to lack faith,
    but I am afraid to trust—
I may be let down.
I do not want to be cowardly,
    but I am afraid to be bold—
I may be labeled as troublesome.
Is that what it means to lead an easy life, O God?
To sidestep any possibility of being hurt,
    to keep aloof from trusting in others,
    to seek shelter from the storm,
        lest the lightning of criticism strike me
        and the thunder of disapproval sound in my ears?
Help me in the spirit of the Lord Jesus Christ
    to pray not for an easy life,
But to be a stronger person.

Let me seek, not tasks equal to my powers,
But powers equal to my tasks.
Let me walk confidently,
   not because of my ability to go in circles,
But because of my steadfast commitment
   to the kind of goals Jesus set.
Let me bring to you, not my proud accomplishments,
But my oftentimes stained,
   occasionally shabby,
   sometimes shining hopes and loves.
Let me come, not just with my morning face and
       eager heart,
But with my tears and aches,
   my doubts and fears.
Let me bring to you the whole of my life
   for healing and renewal.
There is so much to be done,
   yet I am not sure I am capable of being a doer.
Keep me from shrugging it all off,
   and keep me from thinking it is all up to me.

Let me pray to be stronger than I am,
   more faithful and loving.
Let me hold steady and remain alive
   to the joy and excitement of being human.
Let me look to you and to others
   as I go out and walk in the footsteps of the Christ,
      in whose name I pray.   *Amen.*

FOR A TIME OF HELPLESSNESS

Be steadfast, immovable, always abounding in the work of the Lord, knowing that in the Lord your labor is not in vain.

—1 CORINTHIANS 15:58

O God,
I believe you do what you can in us
    and through us
    and with us.
Your Spirit bumps against our contentiousness,
    comes up against our meanness,
    and must deal with our limited understanding
    and our persistent misunderstanding
        of your will and your way.
I am facing a frustrating experience, O Lord,
    frustrating even though
I've seen it many times in the lives of others.
My wife and companion of many years
    can no longer always be by my side.
Her long illness has been debilitating
    and has made an invalid of her.
It is far more bewildering to me than it seems to her.
She appears to go on firmly and calmly,
    steadfast and immovable.
I am grateful for that, O Lord.

You can do so many things for us.
You can straighten us when we start to lean.
We may know times of helplessness,
  but you never do.
You always have the last word.
Right now I hear it deep within my battered spirit.
It sounds like "Courage!"
Thank you. *Amen.*

FOR A TIME OF BROODING

Because the Holy Ghost over the bent
World broods with warm breast and with ah!
bright wings.

—GERARD MANLEY HOPKINS

O Lord, our whole world is bent,
    twisted out of shape,
    tortured into grotesque form and formlessness.
We go down into valleys of prejudice,
    storm up the slopes of war,
    immerse ourselves in rivers of deceit and treachery.
I think about the world you made
    and gave to us human beings,
Saying of it, "It is good."
I think about the way we have bent it out of shape.
We would have broken it into pieces long ago,
    had it not been for the Holy Spirit
    brooding over it and over us.
I must confess it is not very different
    with my little world.
I look at the bent places
    and marvel at your graciousness.
I examine the dents made by bruising experiences,
    some of which I feel pain in recalling.
I know how my life would have broken up
    on more than one occasion,
    save for the Holy Spirit brooding
        "with warm breast and with ah! bright wings."

I thank you, my God, for healing and soothing,
Even for the harsh hammering of the pain
  that more than once removed a dent
  made by heedless, reckless pursuit of my willful way.
Continue to brood over my world
  as you brood over the larger world,
With balm for healing in your wings.   *Amen.*

I AM SO UNPREDICTABLE

Eternal God,
Whose mercy and grace surround me
    whether I see or am blind,
I bring my seeing and my blindness to you now.
For I am a strange mixture of sight and sightlessness.
I saw rain clouds heaped before the wind yesterday,
    and my heart leaped with joy;
Or perhaps I saw a friend of years past
    and coldly turned away.
I heard singing last night,
    and my spirit soared;
Or perhaps I heard singing
    and closed the window of my soul
    to shut out the noise.
I am such an unpredictable creature.
I confess that there is no sure way
    of telling what I may do.
I am a victim of impulse,
    of moods and humors,
    of pressures of the moment
    and whims of the hour.

But through it all, O Lord,
Your mercy and grace surround me
    in my seeing and in my blindness,
    in my hearing and in my deafness.
My hope does not lie in my faithfulness,
    but in yours.

My trust is not in my own stability,
    but in the fact that you are the rock of my salvation;
Of whom shall I be afraid?
I shall not be afraid even of myself
    with my vacillating loyalties
    and my confused commitments.
For I look back across the years
    and am aware that you have done much with me
    and for me,
In spite of my failures, at times, to see.
You have given me moral victories over my baser impulses.
You have given me courage enough
    to get through some dark hour
    when I did not think I would make it.
You have given me someone to love me
    in spite of my unlovableness.
And you have given me someone to love,
    in spite of my fear
        of giving too much of myself.

I have not always acknowledged
    how good life has been much of the time.
I remember vividly the days
    when it went sour.
I treasure the hurts and slights
    and the indignities I have known.
But my life cannot be told
    in terms of such things.
There are old songs to sing again,
    old friends to occupy my heart,
    old faith to renew,
    and old hopes yet to be realized.

Keep me alive to the whole of life, O God,
　　its joys as well as its pain,
　　its beauties as well as its ugliness,
　　its tenderness as well as its toughness.

Touch me where I hurt, O Lord God.
Set me listening to the sounds of life
　　that are all around.
Let me see more clearly the patches of glory
　　that interlace the gray fog of gloom.
Set me to seeing and hearing
　　the signs and sounds of your comings,
　　O Lord,
Through Jesus Christ, in whom I pray. *Amen.*

FOR A TIME OF LOOKING BACK

I will sing a new song to thee, O God.
                                    —PSALM 144:9

O Lord, I have sung the old songs long enough.
I will not forget them,
    but now I must sing a new song.
Another week is done,
    another part of life's story written.
Some weeks are good, filled with joy and pleasure,
    when everything has gone right.
Other weeks are routine—
    nothing bad,
    nothing especially good.
Sometimes the week is long and hard,
    but I have made it through by your grace.
I have managed somehow, and I am grateful.

How can I pay my debt to you for quiet things,
    for steadiness beyond my own strength,
    for faith when I did not know what to believe?
I cannot.

But then, you keep reminding me
    that I do not have to repay you.
Why will I not believe in the extravagant gifts
    you shower upon me?
I ignore the evidences of your immeasurable generosity—
    love I do not deserve,
    grace I cannot merit,
    forgiveness I have no right to demand;

Or I look at you askance or regard you with suspicion.
How can you be God
     and not bat me around?
Why do you not show your muscles?
I try you, defy you, and rebel against you.
Then when I have reached my limit,
I come up against that terrible, flaming love
     that is at the heart of you.
I see the evidences of a love so strong that it cannot be
          downed
     by the virulent hatred of those twisted by life,
A love so straight that it cannot be turned aside
     by the distortions of those who will not understand.

If you are love,
     then what am I?
Am I intended to be a lover?
Why do I get tangled up in hate,
     warped by resentment?
Why do I withdraw from others,
     withhold tenderness?
Am I afraid of being hurt?
I remember how our Lord was hurt,
     his spirit hacked and his body hanged.
Is this the price I may have to pay?
O God, forgive me,
     but I know I am not really up to it,
     at least not all the way.
Maybe, if you will help me,
I can go part of the way some of the time.
I can look less harshly
     upon those I feel have failed or wronged me.

I can be less smug in judging
   those who seem to ruin their lives.
I can ask more questions,
   give fewer dogmatic answers.
I can wait before I speak,
   listen before I condemn.

Another week is done, O Lord, and a new one begins.
It may be routine and ordinary,
   or it may be difficult and painful.
Whatever comes, it is time to sing a new song.
And as I sing it,
I pray the peace that passes all understanding,
   in Jesus Christ our Lord.   *Amen.*

ON SEEING MORE CLEARLY

Eternal God,
Immortal,
Invisible,
Hear me as I pray.
I am not after a vision of glory
   that would dazzle me
Or a tearing aside of the veil
   that would strike me blind.
I ask for much less—
   a glimpse of the Reality
      beyond those things I see and touch daily,
   a hint of the Presence
      that abides through change and circumstance.
I ask not to see forever,
But to see today and, perhaps, tomorrow.
I ask not to see the end of the road—
Sometimes I would be content to see the next few steps.
I stumble rather badly,
   and I grope along.
Sometimes I march boldly ahead,
But I hear no music and have no idea where I am going.
I have no real goal
   and little sense of direction;
I am uneasy,
   and I go around in circles.
Last week was just like the week before.
I find little vitality in life,
   some pleasure,
      but no deep peace and joy.

I would like to see clearly enough
   to discern a purpose and a meaning,
   a direction and a road.

O Lord,
I have closed my eyes now
   because I have been taught
That is the proper way to pray.
Is my problem, in part, due to my failure
   to open my eyes to the world around me?
There are people to see;
   there is beauty to discover,
   even burning bushes
      here and there along the way.
What I see I do not always connect with you.
Yet I know you have fashioned people
   and created beauty
   and set bushes aflame.
If your promises are to be believed,
You are in the midst of this world.
You are the stranger I fail to recognize,
   the love I turn aside,
   the joy I spurn,
   the pain I ignore.
Help me to see,
   if not forever,
At least the present evidences of your Presence.

I need a broader view than I usually have, O God.
I need a vision of your Spirit at work
   in the affairs of people and nations.
I would not presume to read history
   in terms that identify my understanding with your will;

But I can assume that
   where good will is in evidence,
   where loyalty and faith are manifest,
   where concern for all of humanity holds sway,
There is the Spirit of God.
And I can assume that
   when I seek your will as honestly as possible,
   when I bring myself as close to the Spirit of Christ
      as my unruly ego allows,
I shall discover your purpose for me.

So I pray for this nation
   and for its leaders in these turbulent times.
I pray for those who are suffering
   the difficulties of our world.
I pray for myself
   that I may look upon the events of our time with clarity.
Dare I ask to read the newspapers
   and watch the television with the eyes of Jesus?
I know I cannot see as clearly or as compassionately as he,
But I am his follower.

So open my eyes that I may see glimpses of truth
   and evidences of love.
I am your myopic child, I confess,
But you do great things with me
   and for me
      and sometimes through me.
For Jesus' sake. *Amen.*

LORD, I AM SO PETTY

Lord God, Creator of the boundless universe,
   the tossing seas and the outstretched sky,
   the vastness and immensity of space:
I bring you my praise and present my petitions.
I am loaded down with trivia
   and overly concerned with the minutiae of life.
I am burdened with problems that seem so minor
   when I put them out for examination.
I did not finish reading the newspaper
   because the children were demanding attention.
The sports section was missing;
   besides, the baseball teams are all on strike.
The car didn't start;
   after it did, there were no parking places.
I am exasperated and irritated.

But that isn't all.
I am lonely, and I do not know why.
I am fed up for no good reason.
I am devastatingly critical of those I love,
   and the words I speak to them cut and wound.
Even that isn't all.
I despair about our world.
I know flashes of pure dislike for the whole human race
   and, at times, include myself in this contempt.
I indignantly profess my Christianity
   and then act as though I never heard of Jesus Christ.

My sins are venial—
  petty spite, mean resentment, self-justification.
What triviality I unload before you,
O God of the great, the grand, the majestic.

Yet, O God, maybe the trivia I bear
  are not so inconsequential after all.
Maybe you really are concerned
  with the minutiae of my life.
My problems may not be so minor.
For in my loneliness and frustration,
  in my aimless exasperation
  and my poignant inability to love and to be loved,
The great tragedies of humankind are reflected.
You have let me know goodness
  in the ordinary things of life,
To find splendor in everyday experiences,
To laugh at the very absurdities of this world,
  and to transcend its contradictions.
If I can do these things and can respond to life,
If I can rise to each day with gratitude for being alive,
Then I am on the road to meaning.
If I can accept myself
  and respond to someone else's need to be accepted,
Then I am on the road to love.

Clear my vision of life.
Sweep away the clouds that make the skies dark.
I know that in all probability
  they will be back tomorrow,
But for today give me sight and scope.

All these minor things
   bog me down, O Lord.
Perhaps in the vastness of the universe
   they are trivial,
But for me they loom large.

You are God.
You have planted your footsteps in the storm,
   and your spirit rides the wind.
But I need neither storm nor wind.
I need a still, small voice of hope,
   right at the center of my fears.
I need a healing touch,
   a finger laid upon my sore spots.
I need the assurance of the kind of God
   about whom Jesus spoke.
Help me to find you as he did.
No, I cannot find you,
   but you can find me.
So Jesus said;
And with faith in him,
   I come to you. *Amen.*

I NEED REASSURANCE

Life becomes so confusing at times, O Lord.
I am not sure.
I am not really sure what I am for,
I am not really sure whom I am for.
I want to be for Jesus of Nazareth.
I want to be for love.
I want to be a bridge builder.
I want to be a reconciler.
Then there is the hard world in which I live,
    the violent world;
And I end up torn,
    uncertain,
    and confused.
Straighten me out, O Lord.
Teach me how to love.
Teach me how to choose
    to live in the spirit of Jesus,
        son of Mary and Joseph.   *Amen.*

I NEED BROADER VISION

I know, O God,
My prayers should not be for myself alone.
So I pray as I can for other people.
I find it easy to pray for those I love.
I can run through a list of names,
    asking blessings upon those who bear them.
I know people who are ill.
Be with them in their times of pain,
    and sustain them with your healing touch.
I know people who hurt in ways that are not physical
    but may be just as unbearable.
I know people who weep in loneliness at night
    and people who cannot bear the day.
Help me to help them by my words
    and by my accepting silences.
I know I could be more sensitive
    to the needs of others.
Perhaps my prayers for them are lame and limp
    because I fear being chosen by you
        to reach out and touch them.
Perhaps that is why
    I do not always pray for them as I should.

And it is even harder, O Lord,
    to pray for those I do not love—
    for strangers
    and for men and women of different color.
Even here, I am aware
    that your love for the world must include them.

So I lump them all together and say,
"God bless everybody," and have it over.
But I know that will not work.
So I pray as I do for the stranger
and the person who differs from me,
for your children who speak a tongue different from
mine
or use different prayers.
I pray that I may have the grace
to confess my kinship with all people,
And that out of my confession may come a better world.
Let me not forget that Christ died for all people,
That your love embraces all people,
And that in our needs and hopes we are one.

And I am back to myself again, merciful God.
That seems to be where I always end up.
But is that bad?
Are you not concerned with me,
working within me,
molding and making me over?
I believe so and I am grateful,
For I know I need your concern,
your molding and remaking Spirit.
I need daily gifts—
ordinary gifts like steadiness and serenity,
graciousness and courtesy,
balance and humor.
I need these attitudes
because life occasionally batters me,
sometimes buffets me,
and often baffles me.

I need gifts because daily life is so daily.
I pray as I can
And in my praying put myself into your hands,
   gratefully and trustingly,
Through Jesus Christ our Lord.   *Amen.*

FOR A TIME OF UNCERTAINTY

May the God of peace himself sanctify you wholly.
—1 THESSALONIANS 5:23

O God, our Creator,
    hear me as I pray.
Hear my whispering heart and my shouting heart.
Hear me when I believe and when I doubt,
    when I am anxious and when I am indifferent.
Hear me whether I pray in the assurance that you are
    or whether I give expression
    only to tentative, stammering sounds of faith.
I run the gamut of emotions:
    from firm belief to faltering uncertainty,
    from self-confident assurance to wavering insecurity.
Sometimes I think I know who I am and who you are.
Sometimes I am not so sure.
I wish I were.
Hear me, O God, as I pray.

Give me, I ask, a growing sense of life's worth.
Show me, O Lord, how to respond
    to each day's demands and opportunities.
Keep me from bogging down in past failures
    or backing off from future responsibilities.
Keep me from allowing my anxieties to overwhelm me
    and from letting my fears bluff me into immobility.
Help me to see that each day has its own surprises and its
      wonders.

Keep me alert to the possibilities life affords,
and deliver me from sinking into self-pity and
diffidence.
If the troubles of a given day are too much for me,
give me courage to hang on and faith to hang in,
enough to get by.
Keep me from asking too much of life,
But keep me also from the sin of asking too little,
so that I turn sour and unpleasant.

Give me the kind of vision that always encompasses
others,
for I am not alone.
I am part of the family you have created,
I am kin to everyone.
I know I cannot carry all of their burdens,
but I can carry some of them.
I cannot lift the load of suffering from the world,
but I can, at least, set a finger to it.
Guide me in the use of my talents,
my time,
my money,
and my tongue.
Give me joyous relationships with others,
and lead me into helpful meetings day by day.
Let me learn how to speak words of love
loudly enough to be heard,
And words of anger
softly enough to hear what others are saying.
As a member of the Body of Christ
which is the church,
Strengthen my spirit in him
that I may be more like him in attitude and motivation.

I know, O Lord God,
It is far easier to say prayers than to live them,
    to ask for Christ-likeness than to be Christ-like,
    to sing of faith than to live faithfully.
But, then, few of life's rich experiences
    are easily come by.
Love, courage, patience, hope—
    such things are hard to come by.
Keep me, I pray, from ever backing away
    because, at times, life is not easy.
Instead, let me look toward life with steady eyes
    and face this day with hope.
In the spirit of Jesus Christ our Lord. *Amen.*

I MUST BE HONEST WITH MYSELF

Eternal God, Maker of all,
You alone are the ground of my hope,
    the source of my faith in life.
Beyond my comprehension is the wonder of life;
Past my understanding, the sheer mystery of being.
Yet I so often walk with my eyes cast to the ground
    that the stars are strangers to me.
I so often think I have exhausted mystery
    because I have drawn diagrams of the universe.
I so often act as though I have squeezed out wonder
    because I have learned to exploit the world you have
        created.
Even my words of praise have become smooth and worn
    and empty of excitement.
I call upon you, Eternal God,
And my calling carries little of the meaning
    of your eternity of Godhood.
I have carelessly scaled you down in my thoughts.
I worship you as Creator of all people
And unconsciously picture you in my own image
    and after my own likeness.
I indignantly identify you with my values
    and my way of life.
I proclaim you as ground of hope,
But chisel out standing places of my own choosing.
I dare to try to use you and manipulate you.
My religion itself becomes a barrier between us.
Can you break through my false facade
    and confront me on the deep level of my humanity?

Deep within me are places of need.
Secretly, I wonder about myself
  and the meaning of my life.
I am not really sure about tomorrow
  or even today.
Some of my intimate relationships are shaky,
And some of my assumptions about what life is for
  are threatened.
That is why I bristle and bluster
  and shout so loudly at times
About how right I am
  and how wrong others must be.
Do I dare come clean before you and examine myself?
Can my motives bear scrutiny
  and my ambitions bear examination?
Am I as pure as I profess,
  as honest as I pretend?
If I admit my complex, ambiguous self to life,
Will you accept me?
Do I really believe you are the eternal Reality of love
  that endures and creates and re-creates me?
Are you the Creator of all people,
  of the struggling and the bewildered,
  of those whom others deem unworthy?
The Creator of the coward as well as the brave,
  of the groping and the searching,
  as well as of the self-confident and secure?
You have so revealed yourself through Jesus Christ our
      Lord.
Yet I have not always trusted that revelation.

Therein lies my need—
to truly accept you as the ground of hope
For the continuing process of being renewed and
strengthened for life.
I need to let faith in you become the framework
within which I live and move.
Then I know I can believe in life,
revel in its goodness,
endure its evil.
Through faith I can become a child of God
and joint heir of life with Jesus Christ.
Through faith I can love and reach and be free.
Help me, O God, to mean what I say
and say what I mean.
Deliver me from the crippling fear
that makes me avoid an honest confrontation with you.
Walk with me, God,
as I take these steps to a fuller faith. *Amen.*

HERE I AM AGAIN, LORD

Eternal God,
I come to you in my morning prayers.
Each of your children is different,
   unique, even peculiar,
Yet we are all one in our final needs
   and in our ultimate humanness.
We are one in our need
   to belong to you
   and to belong to other people.
We are one in our need to relate our lives
   to some meaning and purpose beyond ourselves.
We are one in our fumbling quest
   for the goodness of life.
But we are different
   in the ways we seek fulfillment of our needs.
Some of us are more fear-filled than others.
We have been wounded, and we smart from our hurts.
Some of us think more highly of ourselves than we
       deserve,
   and some of us think far too little of ourselves.
Some of us have loved and lost,
   and some of us have never really loved at all.
Some of us find satisfaction in our work,
   and some of us feel frustration and emptiness.
Some of us look back with nostalgia,
   and some of us look forward with hope.
Some of us just look around,
   holding our noses to life.
We are different.

But still we are one—
   one in needs,
   one in our humanness,
   one in you.
Perhaps if through you I am able to acknowledge my
      oneness,
   I can help others more.
I can touch others with my hands and my heart.
I can steady someone else.
I can point and beckon and wave and smile.
I can even love others.
I know that is your purpose for me,
Yet I live huddled up and apart,
   bundled in an overcoat of selfishness,
   touching life with the tips of my fingers.
I am too self-conscious to be concerned with others,
   too timid to reach out,
   too uptight to enjoy life.
Perhaps if you will help me
   I can break down some barriers,
   break out of my self-imposed shell of solitude.

I know, O Lord,
There are so many ways in which you can help me,
But I am not sure I want to be helped
   when it comes right down to it.
You have shown me what life can be like in the Lord Jesus,
   and it is frightening.
He kept on going that indomitable way of his,
   and he ended up on a cross.
I have dabbled at love enough to know it can be costly.

Even in my most intimate relationships I can be hurt.
I can be betrayed.
I can be rejected.
I can reach out to a stranger and be rebuffed.
I am small enough of heart
    to wonder at times if it is worthwhile.
Keeping my heart withdrawn is so much safer.
Guarding my feelings is so much less threatening.

But even as I acknowledge my fears, O God,
I am struck with gratitude
    that you did not feel that way about us.
Our Lord was betrayed by a person like us.
He was rejected by his own people.
He did reach out, and his hands were stabbed with nails.
Yet he was big enough of heart to know it was worth it.
I am very grateful.
Where would I be without him?
Where would I be without your grace?
Help me, I pray, in Jesus' name. *Amen.*

Times of Thanksgiving

FOR A TIME OF RECEIVING

What shall I render to the Lord
for all his bounty to me?
I will lift up the cup of salvation
and call on the name of the Lord.
—PSALM 116:12-13

Lord God,
Gift-bearer,
Generous Giver,
I want to receive some of your bounty today.
I cannot absorb it all,
For it is far too plentiful.
I took a deep breath upon waking this morning and said,
    "Thank you for a restful night."
I took in the aroma and flavor of fresh coffee,
    the song of the birds.
I enjoyed the power of bodily vigor
    and the sting of a shower.
The day has hardly begun,
    and I have gifts from your hand.
I know that there are more to come,
    always more to come.

True, O Lord,
There are other things I cannot term bounty,
    at least at first glance.

There are petty annoyances—
  forgetting my glasses,
  phone calls interrupting my concentration,
  details of life I do not want to attend,
  even vexing moments with irritating people.
But those things are all part of the whole,
  and the whole is exciting.
There are all kinds of ingredients in the cup of salvation,
  and I would drain it, dregs and all.
For out of it comes wholeness,
  healing,
  deliverance.
Lord God,
I am grateful for what Jesus called the "abundant life."
Help me receive it and call upon your name.   *Amen.*

FOR A TIME
OF LOOKING TOWARD ETERNITY

Lord God, you made me.
You have set me amid beauty
    and given me a feeling for it.
I am grateful.
I am glad that my heart beats a bit faster
    at the times I feel the beauty around me.
I am grateful for sensuous response to things and people
    I see, hear, touch, smell.
I remember with appreciation moments of sheer physical
        ecstasy.
Such moments always pass,
    and what am I left with?
Memories,
    and a feeling that our greatest raptures
    are dim intimations of an eternal love
    and an eternal beauty.
Does your love surround the love of man for woman,
    friend for friend,
    parent for child?
I think so.
I think when I felt most deeply,
    enjoyed life most intensely,
    even hurt most poignantly,
I was closest to you.
I have always known there was Something,
    Someone,
Beyond my highest experiences of this world.
Now I see through a glass darkly,
But someday I shall see, face to face,
    the grandeur and the glory. *Amen.*

NOT A SPARROW FALLS

*Are not two sparrows sold for a penny? And not
one of them will fall to the ground without your
Father's will.*

—MATTHEW 10:29

O God of sameness and change,
    steadfastness and diversity,
    yesterday and today,
Be very near to me now as I come in prayer.
I am bound to others by so many things—
    memories and shared experiences,
    a common faith and mutual hopes—
Yet we differ from one another in so many ways.
Each brings Sunday cares and Monday needs,
    individual experiences of life
    and personal expectations.
Each brings accumulated anxieties and future fears,
Needs I cannot begin to enumerate.
Yet, O Lord, I pray with the expectation
    that you will sort us out,
For has it not been said that not a sparrow
    falls to the ground without your notice?
I am a falling sparrow, O God.
Take notice of me, I pray;
And if my wings are broken,
    mend me to fly again.

For there is a splendor in our world
for which I am grateful.
There is a vastness to the sky,
a magnificence and a glory,
I am created to appreciate and enjoy.
Give me grace to live, our Sustainer,
to touch and taste and translate time into eternity.
There is a grandeur in my humanness,
too often lost in my absorption
with cheap pleasures and hollow happiness.
There is a privilege in my relationships with others
that I treat lightly,
Engrossed as I so often am
in the emptiness of stroking my ego.
I am grateful for those times
when I am caught up in something
That flings me into contemplation of life's eternal issues:
love and faith,
hope and grace,
the simple glory of being,
and the complex meaning of eternity.
I am thankful that it is hard to live in isolation.
Life keeps breaking in on me.

Glory be to God for a multitude of unexpected things—
a smiling stranger,
a friendly word,
a rainbow,
the fragrance of jasmine,
the hush of prayers.
Glory be to God for the expectations of friends,
the bonds of family,
and the demands I lay upon myself.

Glory be that I cannot sink into self-centeredness
   without pangs of conscience
Or flee to indifference
   without pricks of conscience.
At times I resent being involved.
But in my saner moments I can only say:
   "Thank you, Lord, for not leaving me alone."   *Amen.*

AN EVENING PRAYER

What am I doing here
  before my TV at this hour of the night?
Am I coming in or going out?
Am I left over from the late show?
I find that I cannot sleep
  for I am just one of those night people
  who roam and wander until all hours.
Most people are asleep at this hour,
But many are awake because of their work or their worries,
  their pleasure or their pain.
There is always something special about the middle of the
      night
  and the early hours of the morning.
People pray at night,
  wrestle with God and their own fears at night,
  flee danger at night,
  plan tomorrow at night.
It is a special time.
Whatever my mood I can steady myself
  by the quiet and the still of the night.

I will wait now and be still.
Is there not healing in the night?
I can feel my wounded spirit being soothed,
  my cupful of resentments being overturned,
  and my bagful of disappointments being emptied.
If the cares of the day have been too much for me,
I will let the softness of the night cover them over,
  if only for a few moments.
God is in the night.

Psalm 139 declares,
"If I say, 'Let only darkness cover me,
    and the light about me be night,'
even the darkness is not dark to thee,
    the night is bright as the day;
    for darkness is as light with thee."

I will be still for a moment.
I will let my cup of resentment be refilled with
        thanksgiving,
    my bagful of disappointments be replaced by serenity
        and courage.
I pray that God grants me a good, good night.   *Amen.*

FOR THREE O'CLOCK
IN THE MORNING

In peace I will both lie down and sleep;
for thou alone, O Lord, makest me dwell in safety.
                                              —PSALM 4:8

O God, all hours are beautiful,
Each in its own way.
The sky at five o'clock in the morning is lovely
    with pale traces of dawn
    lying along the edges of the sky.
High noon takes command.
Twilight is sad in a way,
    but beautifully sad.
Light and shadow,
    sun and stars,
    daylight and darkness—
All are beautiful,
    and I am grateful.

I am glad, O God,
    that you have made a world of contrasts,
    that we are bold in the sun
    and silent in the moonlight.
Each hour holds its own contentment,
    each its own revelation.
Thank you for comforting dark and soothing shadow
    wherein I can be alone,
    and yet not alone.

You are near at three o'clock in the morning
    when I let my feelings surface and am myself,
    my crotchety, cantankerous self.
Thank you for accepting me,
Because in feeling acceptance,
    I no longer have to be crotchety.
I can chuckle at my cantankerousness
    and feel relieved of resentment.
At brassy noon do not let me forget
    that three-o'clock-in-the-morning peace.   *Amen.*

FOR A TIME OF GLADNESS

Make a joyful noise to God,
all the earth.
—PSALM 66:1

O Lord God,
    whom I cannot see with my eyes
    or hear with my ears
    or touch with my hands,
You are real and near to me,
    although I am not always conscious of your nearness.
I even doubt your reality at times.
I wonder.
I question.
I grow unsure.
Yet your nearness and your reality
    come surging back to me.

I am most aware that you are
    when I am most aware of life itself.
It may be some moment of heart-wrenching beauty,
    some experience of loving and of being loved,
    some hour of sharing someone else's pain.
It may be a day drenched in joy
    and marked by laughter.
These are times I know—
    without the seeing of eyes
    or the hearing of ears
    or the touching of hands.
These are times I know you are,
And I am glad. *Amen.*

117

I NEED SIMPLICITY

I give you thanks, Merciful God,
That you do not continually dazzle me with angels
    and baffle me with voices from beyond,
For I would be afraid.
I would be coerced;
I would be uncertain;
I would not be human.
But I thank you that you speak to me
    through the ordinary things of life,
That you come to me
    along ordinary paths.
Thanks be to you, O God,
For the revelations of yourself
    in Jesus Christ, our Lord,
And thanks be to you
    for the continued guidance of the Holy Spirit.   *Amen.*

I THANK YOU

Eternal God,
I praise you for being.
I thank you for making me hope that you are,
    feel that you are.
I thank you for the times
    when I have been absolutely and fiercely convinced
    that you are;
And I thank you for those other times when,
    wavering and doubting,
I wonder if you are.
Then some shooting star of faith
    illumines my nighttime spirit
And enables me to take up life again.
I thank you for the little daily graces
    that I take so for granted,
And yet which contain wonders all their own—
    the taste of good food,
    the renewing power of a good night's sleep,
    the pleasant glow I feel in the presence
        of someone I love or just like.
I am ashamed at times
    that I take so many things for granted,
And yet such an attitude may reflect hidden faith
    of which I am not always aware.
This faith believes that,
    regardless of deserving or undeserving,

Life renews itself
 and love reasserts itself.
I am the recipient of both life and love,
 and I am grateful, O Lord.

I pray that my life may be more filled with awareness
 that out of me influence flows
 into the lives of others.
Because I am loved, I can love.
Because I have received, I can give.
Because I am forgiven, I can forgive.
Teach me, O God, more appreciation
 for life's rhythm and flow,
 for receiving and giving,
 for being loved and loving.
Keep me aware each day
 of my interactions with others.
Deliver me from the dark, dull feeling
That I have nothing to contribute.
Make me sensitive to myself
 and to my own worth.
I have been touched by your finger
 and whispered to by your Spirit.
I am your child,
And though I bungle badly at times,
You have never pushed me away.
You help me stand tall and walk straight.
Though I slump now and then and stagger off the path,
You have never let me get so lost
 that I cannot find my way back.

Is it too daring to believe
    that I must matter very much to you?
Or is that not what the Lord Jesus kept affirming?

I am thankful that he came long ago
And thankful that he comes again and again.
Give me the awareness of his daily Presence.   *Amen.*

I HEAR VOICES

Thanks be to you, O God,
For the voices to which I have responded—
   voices of love,
   voices of hope,
   voices calling me to faith.
Thanks be to you, O God,
For the richness of life that has come
   because I rose to the moment
   and responded to the opportunities.
Give to me, O God,
   richer insight,
   greater commitment,
   deeper compassion,
   a more tender heart,
That I may hear your voice
   and the clamorous, glorious voices everywhere
And live in the spirit of our Lord Jesus Christ.   *Amen.*

Times of Beginning

IT'S CHRISTMASTIME AGAIN

O Lord,
I am thankful it's Christmastime again.
The memories come flooding back.
Old hurts and long-dead dreams
    come alive once more.
There are memories I would escape
    and hopes I do not want revived.
Yet even amid such poignant recollections,
There is a heartfelt thankfulness
    that it's Christmastime again
And the story of Bethlehem is retold.
True, much of it has been made gaudy,
    even phony.
My ears have been battered
    with noisy renditions of "Silent Night! Holy Night!"
My mind has been saturated
    with sentimental parodies of the Christmas story.
My spirit has been dulled
    by too much work in preparation.
Yet, deep down, I am glad for this season
    of reminding myself and the world
That God so loved us that he gave us Christmas.

Keep me always mindful
   that it is about Jesus;
That beyond the fatigue and the weariness,
   the gaudiness and the phoniness,
There was a child,
A child whose name was called Jesus,
   who came to save his people from their sins.

Keep me always mindful of the hope
   that rang out on that night of stars and shepherds,
A hope of peace on earth and good will among all people.
He can be lost amid the bustle of Christmastime—
   that I know and confess,
For upon occasion I have lost him.
The hope can be clouded over—
   that I know too,
For often I have forgotten it.
So I prayerfully request a new vision of the Christ
And new hope for the kind of world
   our earth might be. *Amen.*

FOR A TIME OF RENEWAL

Can you lift up your voice to the clouds,
that a flood of waters may cover you?
Can you send forth lightnings, that they may go
and say to you, "Here we are"?

—JOB 38:34-35

Lord of the universe,
Hold on to our world, I pray.
It is our world,
    and we love being a part of it.
We like food and water,
    sunshine and trees,
    and other people.
Yet we keep misusing these things
    and abusing people.
We divide into armed camps
    and wage war on one another.
We exploit the atmosphere and the sea,
    the fertile ground and the rivers
        for our purposes.
You have created the earth and called it good,
    and we have created garbage.
You have created men and women
    to dwell on the face of the earth,
    and we have created gunpowder.
You have made us to love people and use things;
We use people and love things.
We get life turned around.

Straighten us out, Lord—
Straighten us up and straighten us out.
We were made to stand tall,
   to look at the sun
   and to look our brothers and sisters in the eyes.
We were made to walk hills and high roads.
Bring us back in our thinking and our feeling
   to our human destiny
Before we destroy ourselves.

Reveal what I can do
   to make the world a better,
   more beautiful place.
Renew the warm feeling I had
   as I felt your acceptance.
As I think of those I love,
Let my heart reach out toward them.
I must reach across miles in my imagination.
In reconciliation,
   I must reach across gulfs of misunderstanding.
Teach me how to reach.
Give me renewed understanding
   of your long reach toward me in Jesus Christ,
And in that understanding, let me go forth again
   into our world of storm and stress,
   of sunshine and shadow,
To live as Jesus lived.
I come to you in my morning prayers,
   through Jesus Christ our Lord. *Amen.*

HELP ME FIND THE WAY

In the beginning God . . .
—GENESIS 1:1

"In the beginning . . ."
O God, I roll that thought around in my emptied mind.
What does it mean for me?
I find that I keep losing the meaning of life.
It slips away,
   as though my experience of daily existence were a sieve.
I wind up empty and blank.
But if you are always there, O Lord,
Then the meaning cannot really slip away.
I only think it does.
Right now, while I'm cold and quiet and lost,
   you are here.
Always "In the beginning God . . ."
In the beginning of a lifeless cosmos,
In the beginning of a chill gray morning,
   you are forming,
      fashioning,
      creating.

Once upon a time you made a beautiful world.
Now disasters sweep across it,
   disease infests it,
   people despoil and corrupt it.
Are you still making new beginnings, God?
I like to think of it that way, Lord,
   if it is all right with you.

I want to believe that if I reach deep enough into life,
    I find you.
If I plunge my hands into the experience of this day,
    I touch you.
Behind the moon and the stars and the vastness,
    the sweetness of the wind
    and the softness of the rain,
There is your creative spirit.
Yes, Lord, beyond the disasters and disease,
    the pain, the greed, and the sin,
There is the grace-filled presence of your redeeming Spirit.
Help me to think of my world that way.
When I do, I see a cross outlined against a blank sky
And my empty spirit is filled again with gratitude and
        faith. *Amen.*

I NEED TO CHANGE

O Loving God,
Why am I afraid of love,
    forgiveness,
    the compulsion to trust?
Is it because I bungle my relationships so badly,
    because I find it so hard to forgive
    when I have been offended?
Is it because I have proved untrustworthy?
Keep me from reading my inadequate, incomplete
        forgiveness
    and my lack of faithfulness
    into my relations with you, O Lord God.
For I realize, when I think about it,
That I have seen evidences of your faithfulness
    and have felt the tender touch of love and acceptance.
May I let those moments set the tone and tenor
    of my daily experience.

Help me to reach out
    with a gentler hand toward others.
After all my bluster about the need for toughness
I know deep inside that our world
    needs more men and women
    sensitive to the hurts of humankind.
I know that love is healing,
    kindness is helpful,
    courtesy is creative.

I know our homes need more of these virtues,
as do our offices and our schools,
even our churches.
I know that in the affairs of nations
more openness and imagination are needed.
Give the kind of wisdom that is needed
for negotiators for peace
in all parts of the world.
Let them be dogged and determined.
Deliver me from my fears and frustrations
into a better world.

Set me, even me, to the doing of my part.
Give me a hand, Steadfast God,
and teach me when and how
to give a hand to someone else.
Give me a heart, O Lord,
and tell me when
to let others know how I feel.
Give me a mind, O God,
that is not afraid of what is new
or contemptuous of what is old.
May my attitude toward all things
arise increasingly out of my life in Christ Jesus,
in whose spirit I offer this prayer. *Amen.*

FOR A TIME OF BEGINNING AGAIN

He restores my soul.
—PSALM 23:3

O God,
Who breaks down barriers
    and takes away all that separates me
        from true living,
Hear me now as I come to you.
I depend on you to remove the barriers.
I count on you to take away the things
    that separate me from you,
    from others,
    even from myself.
I have tried to make life wholesome and complete—
I have honestly tried.
I have made good resolutions and gone to church.
I have said my prayers and made new beginnings.
I have promised that things would be different.
I want to be more understanding,
    less given to outbursts of temper,
    less ready to blame others for the rifts
        that come in my human relationships.
Sometimes I have managed quite well.
Then all of a sudden I am my old self—
    touchy,
    irritable,
    thoughtless,
    anxious.

I have tried justifying myself.
I have pointed out that,
    after all,
I am rather easy to get along with.
What a pity, I have thought,
    others do not appreciate my worth.
Yes, I am not like others—
    the unrighteous,
    the wicked.

But, when I am finished justifying myself,
I know it will not do.
And somewhere in the secret places of the heart,
I know that in honesty I must say,
    Lord, be merciful to me, a sinner.
Break down the barriers of self-complacency
    that keep me measuring my goodness
    alongside someone else's faults.
Take away the rationalizations
    that keep me from flinging myself fully into life,
    into love,
    into faith.
Help me to be unafraid of being myself.
Deliver me from denigrating my humanness.
You made me,
    and at many points
I have marred what you made.
But no matter what I am or who I am,
    life is not over.

You can remake me where I need remaking,
renew me where I need renewal,
and restore me in the places
    where I have completely broken down.
For you are the God of ever-new beginnings.
Thank you for not always holding up the past before me.
Thank you for saying,
    This is the day the Lord has made.
Rejoice and be glad in it. *Amen.*

I CAN HELP OTHERS

O God, our Creator and Sustainer,
I come to you with this prayer.
Prayer is something to be done,
    harmless and only momentarily helpful at best.
I do not really expect anything.
Prayer is surely a good experience,
    but I have seldom realized its meaning.
Sometimes I am secretly dubious.
Prayer is so meaningful,
    and you are so near.
Sometimes I am filled with wonder and hope.

With such varying moods,
    how can I come to you?
Yet, O Lord, I know you hear me.
I am your child with surging,
    billowing,
    sometimes dominating passions.
At times I feel the frustration of unfulfilled aspirations.
I know I am not very good.
I have flashes of temper
    when I lose control of my tongue.
I have times of despair
    when I lose hold of my goals in life
    and fall into aimlessness.
I have harsh, glaring moments of self-examination
    when I wish I were stronger,
    more loving,
    more open to life.

I am so much like others,
And if only I knew them better,
   they would not be strangers.

There are so many ways
   in which I can live out the spirit of my prayers.
There are other needs I can help meet,
   not only the physical demands of the hungry and
      helpless,
   but the heart-deep needs of the emotionally starved
      and the spiritually weak.
There are friends and members of my family who need me
   and whom I need very much.
Help me to reach others,
   to touch others,
   and to love.
There are ways in which I can reach out
   toward the larger circle of men and women.
I can lift my voice in support of creative tasks
   for the alleviation of injustice.
I can become more aware of broken placcs in society
   that only love can mend.
I can lend my support
   to the uplifting of the wronged and the wrongdoer.
As a child of God,
I know your will is not accomplished by war and suffering.
I know I am called to love my enemies,
   not in splashy, tear-streaked, sentimental ways,
But in the sturdy, courageous ways of persistent good will.
I know love calls for gallantry
   hate is cowardly,
And the barriers behind which I hide are evidences of fear.

So walk beside me today
    that I may see and feel anew my call as a Christian.
I cannot do all that needs doing,
    but I can do something.
I cannot turn the world upside down,
    but I can do more than I have done before.
And now as I wait in prayer,
I remember that it was said long ago
    of the early followers of the Nazarene
That they did turn the world upside down.
Maybe I could too, O Lord.   *Amen.*

Going Forth into the World

I COME FACE TO FACE WITH YOU

Eternal God,
Make these moments of prayer
    a time for genuineness.
I spend so much of my time keeping up appearances—
    let me just be myself for a while.
I do not have to smile now
    If I do not feel like smiling.
I do not have to say anything to you
    I do not mean.
I do not even have to make any promises.
No one but you is looking at me,
    and you see past my smile.
No one but you is listening to my heart-talk,
    and you sort out what I mean from what I say.
I am just who I am and what I am—
    no better, no worse.
I grow tired of being phony so much of the time,
    of professing interest in things
        in which I have no interest,
    of chattering away because I fear the silence,
    of acquiescing in opinions I inwardly detest.
I confess that I relate to others on false bases
    and project distorted images
    because honesty frightens me.

Even with you, O God,
I observe the forms of prayer
    and carefully try to hide my doubts,
    my uncertainties,
    my fears;

I say the things I have been taught.
For a time let me be sincere and open.
I am not very good.
I am not even sure I want to be good.
But I do want to live more abundantly,
    love more completely,
    know more joy in being alive.
Those feelings are genuine, O God.

Touch me now with your Holy Spirit
That I may be made more receptive
    to the abundance that is all around me,
    to the love that is offered me,
    to the joy of being your child.
Give me a sense of appreciation for others
And the discernment to look beyond their pretenses
    to see hearts much like mine.
Give me the persistence to keep seeing beyond the defenses
    by which they protect themselves.
Let me even see through the reserve of strangers,
    for each of us needs others.
Let me not be so easily put off
    by the angry words of those closest to me
    with whom I have quarreled.
Keep me sensitive to the knowledge
    that anger often conceals hurt,
    that aloofness disguises insecurity.

I pray, Loving God,
That today I may carry a new commitment to authenticity
    into all of my relationships in life.
Because I have paused
    and prayed
    and waited through these moments,
May I be more myself than I was,
    more accepted and accepting,
    less given to pretense.
May I go forth to participate to a greater degree
    in the transparent openness of our Lord Jesus Christ,
Who knew people and loved them,
    not always for what they pretended to be
    or even for what they wanted to be,
But for what each person is,
    a child of God.   *Amen.*

KENNETH G. PHIFER served for eighteen years as senior minister of St. Charles Avenue Presbyterian Church in New Orleans. Prior to that time he served congregations in South Carolina and Virginia and in his native state of Tennessee. He was Professor of Homiletics at Louisville Presbyterian Theological Seminary from 1959 to 1965. He earned an A.B. from Centre College in Danville, Kentucky, a B.D. from Louisville Presbyterian Theological Seminary, and an M.A. from Vanderbilt University. In addition he held two honorary doctorates, the D.D. from Hampden-Sydney College in Virginia and the Litt.D. from Centre College in Kentucky. While a student at Louisville Theological Seminary, he was awarded the Walter Kennedy Patterson Fellowship.

Dr. Phifer was a noted author, having written numerous articles in religious journals and several books, including *Tales of Human Frailty and the Gentleness of God, A Protestant Case for Liturgical Renewal, A Star Is Born,* and the best selling *A Book of Uncommon Prayer.*

DOROTHY J. MARCHAL was born in Henderson, Kentucky, and educated in New Orleans. Mrs. Marchal is an elder in her church and a committed volunteer there and in the community. She enjoys a variety of hobbies, including gardening, sewing, cooking, traveling, photography, and reading.

Before retirement, she served as office manager and secretary at St. Charles Avenue Presbyterian Church. For many years she was Dr. Phifer's assistant in manuscript preparation for his various books and published articles.

Following Dr. Phifer's death in 1985, Mrs. Marchal worked tirelessly with his partially completed manuscript, compiling and editing the prayers he had intended to include in a companion volume to *A Book of Uncommon Prayer.* Her efforts have made possible the publication of *A Book of Uncommon Faith.*